HISTORIC COOKERY

HISTORIC COOKERY

AUTHENTIC
NEW MEXICAN
FOOD

Fabiola Cabeza de Baca Gilbert

GIBBS SMITH
TO ENRICH AND INSPIRE HUMANKIND

First Edition
23 22   5 4 3 2

Published by
Gibbs Smith
P.O. Box 667
Layton, Utah 84041

1.800.835.4993 orders
www.gibbs-smith.com

Designed by Debra McQuiston
Printed and bound in China

Gibbs Smith books are printed on either recycled, 100% post-consumer waste, FSC-certified
papers or on paper produced from sustainable PEFC-certified forest/controlled wood source.
Learn more at www.pefc.org.

Library of Congress Cataloging-in-Publication Data

Names: Gilbert, Fabiola Cabeza de Baca, 1894-1991, author.
Title: Historic cookery : authentic New Mexican food / Fabiola Cabeza de Baca Gilbert.
Description: First edition. | Layton, Utah : Gibbs Smith, [2019]
Identifiers: LCCN 2018033191 | ISBN 9781423651611 (hardcover)
Subjects: LCSH: Cooking, American--Southwestern style. | Cooking--New Mexico.
 | LCGFT: Cookbooks.
Classification: LCC TX715.2.S69 G54 2019 | DDC 641.59789--dc23
LC record available at https://lccn.loc.gov/2018033191

CONTENTS

Mrs. Fabiola C. de Baca Gilbert
Home Demonstration Agent Emeritus

PREFACE

Historic Cookery, which first appeared in 1931, may have been the earliest cookbook of New Mexican food to be published. Many of the recipes were heirlooms from the author's family and others were collected from villagers in northern New Mexico. Fabiola Cabeza de Baca Gilbert's cookbook has been credited with the popularization of cooking with chile that led directly to America's love of native New Mexican foods.

In traditional recipes there were no set rules for the preparation of food. The cook was expected to learn the recipes from her relatives. One of the great contributions of *Historic Cookery* is that for the first time the non-native cook was given exact amounts and measures for the preparation of New Mexican food.

The author gives complete recipes for chile sauces, corn dishes, meats, cheese, eggs, and vegetables as well as salads, soups, breads, desserts, and beverages.

Fabiola Cabeza de Baca Gilbert was born near Las Vegas, New Mexico in 1894. She was a noted educator, writer, and home economist.

HISTORIC COOKERY

This little book will help you get acquainted with real New Mexican dishes. New Mexico is a land of changes. Its blue skies of morning may be its red skies of evening. There have been changes in its people, in its customs and culture, and naturally in its food habits. The recipes in Historic Cookery are a product of the past and present—an amalgamation of Indian, Spanish, Mexican, and American. They are typically New Mexican.

Your experiments in New Mexican cookery can be fascinating. Remember, though, that when you try any of these recipes, you should be prepared to spend plenty of time. *Guisar,* which has no exact English equivalent, is the most popular word in the native homemaker's vocabulary. Roughly translated, it means to dress up food, perhaps only by adding a little onion or a pinch of oregano; good food always deserves a finishing touch. Food must never taste flat, but it will—if it's not *guisado*.

In recent years, New Mexican foods have become increasingly popular. That's why you may have to stand in line when you eat in restaurants that specialize in New Mexican dishes. Why this new popularity? The principal reason, of course, is that the food is good. Another is that recent research has proved that many of our basic foods—chile, beans, purslane, lamb's quarters, goat's cheese, and whole grain cereals, for example—are highly nutritious.

Try the recipes. And when you do, think of New Mexico's golden days, of red chile drying in the sun, of clean-swept yards, outdoor ovens, and adobe houses on the landscape. Remember the green valleys where good things grow. And think too of families sitting happily at the tables—because good food and good cheer are natural *compadres* and because, as the Spanish proverb says, a full stomach makes a happy man. *Buen provecho, amigos*.

SALSAS DE CHILE
(CHILE SAUCES)

Since many New Mexican dishes require a little chile sauce, it is appropriate to explain its preparation first. Ground or powdered chile may be purchased, but care must be taken that the product is pure. Sauce prepared from chile pods is more satisfactory.

Chile Sauce I

Chile Sauce A

3 tablespoons fat
2 tablespoons flour
1 clove garlic, chopped

8 tablespoons chile powder
2 cups hot water
1 teaspoon salt

Melt fat, add flour and garlic. Brown well. Add chile powder and blend. Slowly add water. Stir in salt and cook until thick.

Chile Sauce B

24 chile pods
1 quart boiling water
1 teaspoon salt
1 tablespoon fat

1 tablespoon minced onion
1 clove garlic, chopped
1 teaspoon oregano

Wash chile pods; remove stems, seeds, and white veins. Put in a kettle and pour boiling water over them. Cook until tender. Pass through a food mill or fruit press until all the pulp has been removed from the skins. Add as much of the water in which it was boiled as is needed for desired consistency. (A good consistency for chile is that similar to tomato sauce.) Put on stove, add salt, fat, onion, garlic, and oregano. Bring to a boil.

Note The use of your electric blender for making chile sauce will save you time, and you will get more sauce from the pods than by any other method.

To make Remove stems, seeds, and veins from pods. Place pods in a warm oven (200 degrees F), being careful that chile pods do not scorch, for about 10 minutes, stirring often and leaving oven door open. Remove chile pods from oven, add enough warm water to cover, and let soak for 15 minutes. Place chile pods and seasoning in the blender and add enough water to cover, leaving about one inch space or more in the glass container. Blend for 2 minutes. If sauce is too thick, add more water, if there is space, and blend one minute or until skins disappear completely. Remove from container and add enough water to give desired consistency.

Sixteen large chile pods will yield about 1 quart of sauce. For this amount, use 1 clove garlic, 1 tablespoon chopped onion, 1 teaspoon salt, and 1 teaspoon oregano for seasoning.

Chile Sauce with Tomatoes II

1 tablespoon chopped onion
2 cloves garlic, chopped
3 tablespoons olive oil or fat
6 medium-size fresh tomatoes

8 tablespoons powdered chile or
   1 cup Green Chile V (page 17)
1 tablespoon oregano
1 teaspoon salt
1 teaspoon vinegar

Fry onion and garlic in oil or fat. Add tomatoes; cook until thick. Add chile and seasoning. (1 cup Chile Sauce I B (page 14) may be used instead of powdered chile.) Cook for 5 minutes.

Sweet Chile Sauce III

2 quarts ripe tomatoes
4 pods green chile
1 pod red chile
4 small onions
1 tablespoon salt

$\frac{1}{2}$ teaspoon ginger
6 tablespoons brown sugar
1 teaspoon cinnamon
3 cups cider vinegar

Grind tomatoes, chiles, and onions. Add salt, ginger, brown sugar, and cinnamon and boil until tender. Add vinegar and cook for 5 minutes. Put into sterilized jars and seal. Lettuce and Sweet Chile Sauce make good sandwiches.

Salsa Picante IV (Hot Sauce)

2 large fresh tomatoes
6 green chiles
1 clove garlic
½ cup chopped onion

2 tablespoons vinegar
1 teaspoon cayenne pepper
1 teaspoon cinnamon
Salt

Peel tomatoes. Roast and peel chiles, remove stems and seeds, or use canned green chile. Grind tomatoes, chiles, garlic, and onion together until fine. Add vinegar and spices.

Green Chile V

Wash chile pods; snip ends. Place on top of stove, in broiler, or in oven. Brown on all sides. When done, place in pan, cover with wet cloth, and let steam for 10 minutes. Peel, using long strokes. Remove stems. Take out seeds by holding pod in one hand, stem pointing down, squeezing it between the fingers of the opposite hand. Chop, add salt, garlic, and chopped onion. Serve as a relish.

CORN DISHES
(CORN DISHES)

Many varieties of corn may be used in corn dishes. When nixtamal is to be used for pozole, the best variety is the white flint or the concho. For tortillas, blue native and concho are adaptable. White flint and concho are the best varieties for tamales. Try the blue corn for variety in making tamales.

Nixtamal (Lime Hominy)

**2 heaping tablespoons
  powdered lime
2 quarts water
1 quart dry corn**

Dissolve lime in water. Add to corn. Stir well. Place in granite or enameled kettle.
Cook until hulls loosen from the kernels. Remove from fire; drain off lime water.
Wash in cold water until lime is removed and the water comes out clear.

Note *Masa* for tortillas and tamales is made from nixtamal.

Tortillas de Nixtamal (Lime Hominy Tortillas)

Corn tortillas may be used for making enchiladas, tacos and tostadas, or as bread with Mexican and New Mexican foods. These may be bought already prepared in cans or packages.

The lime hominy described on the facing page may be used to grind into masa for the tortillas. The hominy should only be washed once, when the hulls are loosened from the kernels. Pass hominy through medium knife of food chopper several times. If too dry, add enough water so that the dough or masa can be held together. Shape into balls of desired size. Place one end of a damp towel over a bread board, put ball of masa on the towel, cover with the other end of the damp towel, and press down with another small board until tortilla is about $1/8$-inch thick. Cook on both sides on a slightly greased griddle.

Variation Prepared meal called *harinilla* may be bought and used in making corn tortillas. To make tortillas from harinilla, proceed as follows: Take 2 cups of harinilla and add enough boiling water to make a medium hard dough—just enough to handle and shape into balls. Proceed as for tortillas made of nixtamal.

Enchiladas

After the tortillas are made, fry them in hot deep fat. Some people like their enchiladas rolled. To do this, make tortilla about 6 inches in diameter. Fry. Fill half of the tortillas with grated cheese and onion cut into small pieces. Add Chile Sauce I or II (page 14 or 16), fold the tortilla over the filling, and turn edge under.

The New Mexican way of making enchiladas follows: Fry tortilla in deep fat, immerse in chile sauce, place on platter, sprinkle with grated cheese, and chopped onion. Cover with Chile Sauce I or II, and place another tortilla on top: repeat the process: then pour enough chile sauce over them to cover tortillas. Two tortillas make one serving. A fried egg may be served on top of each enchilada.

Enchiladas Verdes (Green Enchiladas)

10 green chiles
2 cups cooked tomatoes
2 tablespoons fat
1 egg
1/2 cup cream

Salt, to taste
8 corn tortillas
1 cup grated cheese
1 cup chopped onion
Lettuce leaves

Roast and peel green chiles, remove stems and seeds, or used canned green chile. Chop chiles fine, add tomatoes and fry in fat. Beat egg, add cream and salt. Mix with chile and tomatoes and cook until thick.

Fry tortillas in deep fat, fill each tortilla with cheese and onion and roll. Serve on lettuce leaves topped with the green chile sauce.

Pozole de Nixtamal

2 cups Lime Hominy (page 20)
6 cups water
1 pound pork ribs or other boiling
   hog meat
1/2 pound pork rind

4 dried red chile pods
2 teaspoons salt
2 cloves garlic, chopped
2 teaspoons oregano
2 teaspoons saffron

Cook the hominy in water until the kernels begin to burst; then add meat, pork rind, and chile pods (seeds and stems removed). When nearly done, add salt, garlic, oregano, and saffron.

Note If the pressure cooker is used to cook the pozole, cook the hominy without pressure until the kernels begin to burst; then add meat and chile pods. Cook at 15 pounds pressure for 30 minutes. Remove lid from cooker; add salt, garlic, and oregano; cook uncovered for 25 minutes.

Pozole de Chicos (Green Corn)

Green corn steamed and dried on the cob and then shelled is called *chicos*. Chicos may be substituted for hominy in Pozole de Nixtamal. The chicos do not burst; they merely swell when cooked.

Chicos Quebrados (Cracked Chicos)

1 cup chicos
2 tablespoons fat
½ small onion, chopped

1 clove garlic, chopped
1 cup chile sauce or 4 tablespoons
   powdered chile
1 teaspoon salt

Crack dry chicos in food chopper. Cook until tender in enough water to cover. Melt fat; fry onion and garlic; add drained chicos, chile sauce, and salt. Add enough of the liquid in which the chicos were cooked to make it of a thick consistency.

Tamales

Tamales may be made from homemade nixtamal. If this is used, wash the nixtamal more thoroughly than for tortillas. Grind very fine.

There are commercially prepared meals, one is called harinilla and others by different trade names.

**6 cups masa or commercially
   prepared meal
3 ½ cups water**

**2 cups lard
2 teaspoons salt**

If masa made from nixtamal is used, it may need less water than the prepared meals.

Add water to meal. Beat lard until creamy and add to masa. Beat to the consistency of thick cream. The electric beater may be used. Season with salt.

Prepare corn husks by trimming, washing, and soaking in warm water.

Prepare Carne con Chile (page 33). The amounts given will yield enough for the 6 cups of masa. Be sure the Carne con Chile is of thick consistency so that it will adhere to masa and not be runny.

Spread each husk with 2 tablespoons of masa and 1 heaping tablespoon of Carne con Chile. Fold sides together, bring top and bottom of husk together and tie with corn husk strings. Steam for 40 minutes or cook under pressure for 20 minutes at 15 pounds. Makes 5 to 6 dozen tamales.

CARNES, AVES DE CORRAL Y PESCADO
(MEATS, POULTRY, AND FISH)

Natives of New Mexico rarely serve roasts, steaks, and chops. When meat is freshly butchered, the New Mexican cook may take a piece of liver, strips of round steak, the heart or kidneys and put them in the oven or broiler. However, meat is seldom prepared without the addition of chile, potatoes, or vegetables.

With the new knowledge of nutrition, we have learned that the organs of the animals are good sources of different vitamins. The New Mexican families learned from colonial times how to use every part of the animal. They eat the blood, stomach, intestines, liver, kidneys, and glands.

As with meat, the New Mexican cook rarely serves poultry without the addition of a sauce or vegetable.

Albondigas (Meat Balls)

1 ½ pounds round steak or other
   meat suitable for grinding
6 tablespoons blue corn meal or
   1 cup bread crumbs
2 eggs, beaten

2 cloves garlic, chopped
2 teaspoons ground coriander seed
2 teaspoons salt
1 teaspoon pepper
½ onion, chopped fine

Grind meat. Add other ingredients and mix well. Shape into balls of desired size.

Soup

4 tablespoons fat
2 tablespoons flour
4 cups hot water

2 teaspoons dried mint leaves
1 teaspoon saffron
Salt

Melt fat and brown flour in it. Add water and seasonings. When it starts boiling, drop the meat balls into it and cook until meat is well done. Serves 8.

Pierna de Carnero Asada (Roast Leg of Mutton)

1 leg of mutton (4 pounds)
2 tablespoons fat
2 teaspoons salt
1 teaspoon pepper
2 cups canned tomatoes

1 small onion, sliced
2 cloves garlic, chopped
1 bay leaf
6 small carrots

Rub leg of mutton with fat, salt, and pepper. Roast uncovered for 45 minutes. Take out, add tomatoes, onion, garlic, bay leaf, and carrots. Cover and bake until done. Serves 8.

Carne Adobada (Cured Pork)

2 teaspoons salt
3 cloves garlic, chopped
2 tablespoons oregano

1 quart Chile Sauce I B (page 14), uncooked
5 pounds pork strips (any tender cut)

Add salt, garlic, and oregano to chile sauce. Place strips of pork about 6 inches long, 2 inches thick, and 2 inches wide in the chile sauce. Let stand for 24 hours. It may be kept in this sauce until it is all used.

To prepare Take out as much meat as desired for preparation. Cut in small pieces. Fry in small amount of fat. Add chile sauce enough to cover, and cook until done, adding chile sauce as needed to keep from drying.

If desired, the strips of meat may be dried and used later. To do this, take out strips from the sauce and hang in the shade to dry. When dried, store in a dry, cool place. Later, before preparing it, pound until well-shredded. Fry in small amount of fat. Add enough chile sauce to keep from drying. Cook until meat is tender.

Carne con Chile Colorado (Meat with Red Chile)

Round steak cut in small cubes and browned in hot fat makes very good carne con chile. Boiling meats, however, impart a particular flavor which is not obtained otherwise. Avoid using meat with a great deal of fat. Genuine carne con chile must never have a greasy film.

1 ½ pounds boiling meat	1 teaspoon salt
2 tablespoons fat	1 teaspoon oregano
2 cups chile sauce or 8 tablespoons powdered chile	1 clove garlic, chopped
	1 cup meat stock or tomatoes

Cook meat until tender but not too well-done. Cut into small cubes. Fry in fat until brown. Remove from fire. Add chile sauce or powdered chile. Season with salt, oregano, and garlic. Add meat stock or tomatoes. Cook for half an hour. If chile powder is used, increase the meat stock or tomatoes by 1 cup.

Carne con Chile Verde (Meat with Green Chile)

1 ½ pounds boiling meat
2 tablespoons fat
1 cup canned green chile or Green
   Chile V (page 17)

1 teaspoon salt
2 cups meat stock or tomatoes

Cook meat until tender. Cut into cubes. Fry in hot fat until brown. Remove from fire. Add chopped green chile, salt, and meat stock or tomatoes. Cook slowly for ½ hour.

Estofado (Sweet Stew)

1 ½ pounds stew meat
4 cups water
4 tablespoons chopped onion
4 tablespoons fat
1 cup raisins

1 teaspoon cinnamon
1 square of chocolate or
   4 tablespoons cocoa
1 teaspoon salt
1 clove garlic, chopped

Cut meat into cubes and boil in water until tender. Fry onion in fat until done. Remove onion and add meat. Fry until brown. Add 2 cups meat stock, raisins, cinnamon, chocolate or cocoa, and salt. Add onion and garlic. Cook for ½ hour.

Carne de Olla (Stew)

1 ½ pounds stew meat (lamb, kid, veal, or beef)
2 quarts water
1 cup green beans, cut into pieces
6 pieces of corn on the cob, cut in 2-inch pieces
4 tiny squashes
5 squash blossoms
2 tablespoons green onion tops
2 tablespoons green garlic tops
2 tablespoons coriander leaves
2 teaspoons salt

Cook meat until tender. Strain stock. If it has boiled down, add water to bring it back to 2 quarts. Add vegetables. Cook until beans are tender. Add meat, squash blossoms, and seasonings. Cook ½ hour. Serve.

Chiles Rellenos (Stuffed Green Peppers)

1 pound boiling meat
4 cups water
1 teaspoon salt
1 cup raisins
2 teaspoons ground coriander seed
½ teaspoon ground clove
2 cloves garlic, chopped
2 tablespoons chopped onion
12 green chiles

Batter

1 cup flour
1 teaspoon baking powder
½ teaspoon salt
1 cup milk
2 eggs, slightly beaten

Sauce

4 tablespoons fat
4 tablespoons flour
1 cup meat stock
1 cup tomato sauce

Cook meat. When done, grind and add salt, raisins, spices, garlic and onion. Add enough of the meat stock to moisten. Cook until thick.

Wash chile pods. Place on top of stove, in broiler, or in oven. Brown on all sides. When done, place in pan, cover with wet cloth, and let steam for 10 minutes. Peel, using long strokes. Slit chiles in center; remove seeds; stuff with meat filling.

Batter

Sift the flour with the baking powder and salt. Blend the milk and eggs together; add to flour mixture. Dip stuffed peppers into batter using a large spoon; drop into hot oil or fat and fry until brown. Serve with tomato sauce if desired.

Sauce

Melt fat and brown flour in it. Add meat stock and tomato sauce. Cook for 5 minutes. Pour sauce over stuffed chiles. Cover and let stand over very low heat until ready to serve.

Menudo (Tripe)

The New Mexican cook cleans the tripe as it comes from the newly butchered animal—beef, kid, veal, or lamb. Tripe already cleaned can be bought in the market.

Wash stomach well. Pour boiling water over it and let stand for 10 minutes. Scrape thoroughly with a knife, until all scum is removed and the tripe is white.

1 quart cleaned tripe, cut in 1-inch pieces	1 chile pod
2 quarts water	2 teaspoons oregano
1 small onion	2 teaspoons salt

Cook tripe in water until tender. Add onion and chile pod from which the stems and seeds have been removed. Add oregano and salt to taste. Cook ½ hour or until the soup becomes medium thick.

Morcilla (Blood Pudding)

When an animal is being butchered, the New Mexican cook goes out with a pail in hand to catch the blood as the neck of the animal is cut. She immediately works out the clots before the blood gets cold.

1 quart hog's blood
4 tablespoons fat
1 small onion, chopped
1 clove garlic, chopped
1 cup raisins

$^1/_2$ cup piñon nuts, shelled
1 teaspoon oregano
1 teaspoon dried mint
2 teaspoons salt

Fry blood in the fat; add onion and garlic. Stir constantly until the blood is well-scrambled. Add raisins, which have been soaked and drained. Cook for $^1/_2$ hour. Add piñon nuts and seasonings. Cook slowly for another $^1/_2$ hour.

Morcilla de Cabrito (Kid's Blood Pudding)

2 cups small intestines, cleaned and
   cut in pieces
1 quart kid's blood
2 cups kid's tripe (third stomach) cut
   in pieces
4 tablespoons fat

1 medium onion, chopped
2 cloves garlic, chopped
1 teaspoon oregano
1 teaspoon dried mint
2 teaspoons salt

The intestines are cleaned by pouring water in them and squeezing through fingers
to remove all dirt.

Fry blood, tripe, and intestines in fat. Add onion and garlic and cook for $1/2$
hour. Add seasonings and cook until intestines are done. It may be necessary
to add water to keep from drying.

Riñones (Kidneys)

5 or 6 kidneys (lamb or kid)
4 tablespoons butter
1 small onion, chopped
2 tablespoons parsley

½ cup white wine
1 small can mushrooms
1 cup tomato sauce
Salt and pepper

Remove fat and skin from kidneys and slice thin. Fry in butter for a few minutes. Add onion and parsley, and cook until onion is done. Add wine and cook for 5 minutes. Mix mushrooms with tomato sauce and add to kidneys. Season and cook until kidneys are well-done. Place on serving dish and garnish with fried ham and sliced hard-cooked eggs

Panza de Cabrito Rellena (Stuffed Kid's Stomach)

The kid's stomach, which has been cleaned, may be stuffed with the Morcilla (page 39) and sewed up with twine. Place stuffed stomach in a steamer and cook for 2 hours. When done, slice and serve.

Pipian de Lengua (Tongue Fricassee)

Cook a beef tongue until tender. Remove skin and slice.

Sauce

½ cup pumpkin seeds
3 tablespoons fat
1 clove garlic, chopped

2 cups water or stock from boiled
  tongue
1 teaspoon salt
1 teaspoon coriander seed

Roast pumpkin seeds; remove skins and grind into a powder. Melt fat; add powdered pumpkin seeds, garlic, liquid, and seasonings. If desired, chile powder or chile sauce may be added for seasoning. Add the cooked tongue to this sauce and cook slowly for 30 minutes. Any kind of cooked meat may be used instead of tongue.

Arroz con Pollo (Rice with Chicken)

1 (4- to 5-pound) cooking chicken
2 teaspoons salt
1/4 teaspoon pepper
2 tablespoons olive oil
12 ripe olives, sliced

1 small onion, chopped
2 1/2 cups canned tomatoes
1 teaspoon chile powder
1 cup rice

Cut chicken in pieces as for frying. Sprinkle with salt and pepper. Heat oil. Add olives, onion, tomatoes, chile powder, and chicken. Cover and cook until chicken is almost done. Add rice to chicken mixture. Add 1 teaspoon salt to 2 1/2 cups boiling water and pour over rice. Cover and cook until rice is tender and moist, not dry. Serves 6.

Pepitoria de Gallina (Chicken Fricassee)

1 fricassee chicken
Flour
½ cup oil or butter
1 small onion, chopped
1 teaspoon saffron
½ teaspoon nutmeg

Salt and pepper
1 teaspoon oregano
1 teaspoon mint
1 cup white wine
1 cup chicken stock

Joint the chicken. Boil until tender; dredge in flour; fry in oil or butter until brown; add onion, spices, and herbs. Add wine and stock, and cook until sauce thickens. Serve with garnish of green peas and parsley.

Pollo Frito (Fried Chicken)

1 frying chicken, cut in pieces
Flour
½ cup oil or butter
Salt
2 tablespoons chopped onion
2 tablespoons parsley

1 clove garlic, chopped
1 sweet green pepper, chopped
3 tablespoons flour
1 cup water
2 tablespoons lemon juice

Dredge chicken in flour. Fry in oil or butter until brown; salt and take out. In the oil or butter, fry onion, parsley, garlic, and pepper. Brown the flour, and add water and cook until thickened. Salt to taste. Add lemon juice. Pour this sauce over chicken and serve.

Gallina Rellena (Stuffed Fowl)

This dish is served on very rare occasions, such as Christmas, New Year's, Easter, or at a banquet.

1 (12- to 15-pound) roasting fowl	1 teaspoon coriander seed
½ pound butter	1 teaspoon cinnamon
1 pound cooked ground beef	½ teaspoon ground cloves
2 cups raisins	1 cup meat stock
½ cup shelled piñon nuts	Salt
2 squares chocolate	½ cup red wine

Clean fowl as usual. Rub inside with butter. To the ground beef add raisins, nuts, melted chocolate, spices, meat stock, and salt. Cook until thick. Add wine and let boil for 10 minutes. Stuff fowl as usual and cook until tender.

Bacalao (Codfish)

1 pound codfish
6 tablespoons oil or fat
1 small onion, cut in rings
2 cloves garlic, chopped
3 teaspoons chile powder

¼ cup water
1 cup tomatoes
Salt
1 cup bread crumbs

Soak codfish and wash well. Cut in pieces. Sauté onion in oil. Add garlic. Mix chile with water. Place codfish in buttered casserole, adding onion, chile, and tomatoes. Salt. Sprinkle with buttered bread crumbs and bake in a moderate oven until fish is done.

Pescado Frito (Fried Fish)

6 slices white fish
½ cup flour or corn meal
½ cup oil or fat

Sauce
2 cloves garlic, chopped
1 small onion, chopped

3 tablespoons olive oil
1 cup tomato sauce
2 red chile peppers (stems and
  seeds removed)
1 teaspoon oregano
2 tablespoons vinegar
Salt

Dip fish in flour or corn meal. Fry in oil or fat until brown. Serve with sauce.

To prepare sauce, fry garlic and onion in oil. Add tomato sauce and chile peppers. Season with oregano, vinegar, and salt. Serve over fried fish.

Pescado Relleno (Stuffed Fish)

2 pounds halibut
2 tablespoons fat
1 small onion, chopped
2 cloves garlic, chopped
3 tomatoes, chopped

3 eggs, beaten
1 cup chopped almonds
1 teaspoon chopped parsley
Salt

Clean fish and remove bones. Melt fat, and sauté onion and garlic. Add chopped tomatoes, stir in eggs, and cook until eggs curdle. Add nuts, parsley, and salt. Stuff fish with egg mixture. Place in cheese cloth and tie. Bake or broil in greased dish.

Trucha Frita (Fried Trout)

1 large or several small trout
½ cup oil or fat
1 small onion, chopped
1 tablespoon vinegar

1 teaspoon parsley
1 tablespoon butter, melted
1 clove garlic, chopped
½ lemon, sliced

Clean trout. Fry fish, add onion, and cook until onion is done. Add vinegar to parsley, melted butter, and garlic. Pour over fish and onions, and garnish with fresh parsley and lemon slices.

Cocktail de Camaron (Shrimp Cocktail)

3 tablespoons catsup
3 tablespoons chopped celery
1 tablespoon lemon juice
½ teaspoon red chile powder or
  2 drops Tabasco sauce

1 tablespoon Worcestershire sauce
½ teaspoon salt
Canned or fresh shrimp

Mix sauce ingredients thoroughly. Place canned or fresh shrimp in cocktail glasses. Add 1 tablespoon of the sauce for each serving. Top with an olive.

Torrejas de Camaron (Shrimp Fritters)

3 eggs
1 cup canned or ½ cup dry shrimp
4 tablespoons flour
½ teaspoon baking powder

2 teaspoons salt
Fat
3 cups Chile Sauce I (page 14),
   of choice

Separate eggs, beat whites until stiff, beat yolks, and add to whites. Add shrimp, cut fine or ground. Mix well; add flour sifted with baking powder and salt. Drop by tablespoonful into hot fat. Brown on both sides; make Chile Sauce I, and drop fritters into hot sauce. Let them stand in sauce until well-soaked. Serve.

QUESO Y HUEVOS
(CHEESE AND EGGS)

Cheese from goat's milk has been popular in New Mexico since colonial times. Anyone who has once tasted it in the different dishes can never quite get used to another kind of cheese. Cheese making is not difficult and can become a very interesting experiment. Cow's milk can be substituted in the following recipes.

If one desires to buy the cheese, any of the varieties in the market may be used, depending on individual taste.

Queso Fresco (Native Fresh Cheese)

1 gallon sweet milk
4 Junket tablets or $1/10$ rennet tablet

Warm the milk to 90 degrees F. Dissolve Junket or rennet tablets in 4 teaspoons water. When dissolved, stir thoroughly into the warm milk. Let stand for $1/2$ hour. When set, cut with hand or with knife into small pieces. Remove as much of the whey as possible. Pour curd into a small cloth bag, and let drain until all whey has disappeared.

Requeson (Whey Cheese)

Take the whey left over from the Queso Fresco and place in a kettle over low fire. As it boils, add sweet milk, not to exceed 2 cups for every gallon of whey. Add milk a little at a time, stirring only to keep from sticking. The milk helps to make a soft curd but may be omitted. The curd, which is the milk sugar, comes to the top. This may be skimmed off as it forms or strained after whey has boiled down.

Chiles Rellenos con Queso
(Chiles Stuffed with Cheese)

Green chiles
Grated cheese, of choice

Batter

1 cup flour
1 teaspoon baking powder
½ teaspoon salt
1 cup milk
2 eggs, slightly beaten

Wash chile pods. Place on top of stove, in broiler, or in oven. Brown on all sides. When done, place in pan, cover with wet cloth, and let steam for 10 minutes. Peel, using long strokes. Slit chiles in center; remove seeds. Stuff each chile with 2 heaping tablespoons grated cheese. Dip in batter.

Batter

Sift the flour with the baking powder and salt. Blend the milk and eggs together; add to flour mixture. Dip stuffed peppers into batter using a large spoon; drop into hot oil or fat and fry until brown.

Chile Verde con Queso (Green Chile with Cheese)

Dried green chile is best, but canned chile may also be used—one cup canned green chile or its equivalent of the dry product after it has been soaked.

3 tablespoons chopped onion
1 clove garlic, chopped
3 tablespoons fat

1 cup canned green chile
1 cup thinly sliced cheese
1 teaspoon salt

Fry onion and garlic in fat. Add coarsely chopped green chile and sliced cheese. Add salt. Cook over slow fire until cheese is melted.

Huevos Rancheros (Eggs with Chile)

2 eggs
2 tablespoons fat

1 cup Chile Sauce with Tomatoes II
(page 16)

Break eggs. Drop into fat; cover and cook slowly until white is done. Serve on plate and pour hot chile sauce over them. The eggs may be poached in the chile sauce if desired.

Chongos (Cheese Twists)

2 Junket tablets
2 ½ quarts warm fresh milk
6 egg yolks

4 cinnamon sticks
2 cups sugar

Dissolve Junket tablets in 1 tablespoon milk; add to rest of milk. Beat egg yolks. Add to milk. Strain. Let set until milk clabbers. Cut clabber with a knife in large pieces. Place a piece of stick cinnamon on each piece of curd. Add sugar and place over low heat and cook for about 1 hour or until syrup thickens. Cool and serve with the syrup. If the syrup does not thicken enough and to prevent overcooking of cheese, remove cheese and boil syrup until thick.

Sopa Seca de Arroz (Dry Rice Soup)

4 tablespoons fat
½ small onion, cut fine
1 clove garlic, chopped

2 cups cooked rice
2 teaspoons saffron
2 hard-cooked eggs

Melt fat, fry onion and garlic, and add rice and saffron. Pour into a serving dish and garnish with hard-cooked eggs.

Quesadillas (Cheese Turnovers)

There are many varieties of quesadillas, but the following is the most common.

1 ½ cups native cheese
2 eggs
½ cup sugar
1 teaspoon cinnamon
1 teaspoon salt
2 tablespoons milk

Masa (Dough)

1 ½ cups flour
1 teaspoon baking powder
1 teaspoon salt
8 tablespoons shortening
4 to 6 tablespoons water

Grate cheese finely; add beaten eggs, sugar, cinnamon, salt, and enough milk to make a thick paste.

Masa (Dough)

Sift flour with baking powder and salt. Cut in shortening. Add water, working quickly so as not to over mix the dough. Roll out dough $1/8$ inch thick. Cut in rounds about 4 inches in diameter. Place 2 tablespoons of cheese filling in each piece of dough; fold over and turn edges. Bake in hot oven until well-browned.

Torrejas (Egg Fritters)

3 eggs
2 tablespoons bran

1 teaspoon salt
6 tablespoons fat

Separate eggs. Beat whites until stiff but not dry. Beat yolks and add to whites. Add bran and salt. Drop by tablespoons into hot fat. Drain on absorbent paper.

Torrejas con Chile (Chile Fritters)

Make 2 cups Chile Sauce I A (page 14). Drop egg fritters into hot chile sauce. Set on back of stove until ready to serve.

Tortilla Española (Spanish Omelet)

4 medium potatoes
6 tablespoons fat
1 teaspoon salt

1 teaspoon pepper
6 eggs
¼ cup milk

Cut potatoes in small cubes. Fry in fat until done and well-browned. Add salt and pepper. Beat the eggs well; add milk and pour over the potatoes, stirring while they curdle. Cook over a slow fire. Turn and cook on other side, being careful not to overcook. Serves 6.

VEGETALES Y ENSALADAS
(VEGETABLES AND SALADS)

Chícharos Maduros (Dried Mature Peas)

1 cup dried peas
5 cups water
1 onion, sliced
1 clove garlic, chopped

2 tablespoons fat
1 teaspoon oregano
1 teaspoon ground coriander seed
Salt, to taste

Soak peas overnight. Cook in boiling water. When cooked for 1 hour, skim off skins which come to the top. Add onion and garlic; cook until tender and water has boiled down. Mash and add fat, oregano, coriander, and salt. Cook long enough to bring out the seasonings.

Chícharos Verdes (Green Peas)

2 cups shelled fresh peas
Enough water to cover peas
1 teaspoon salt

2 tablespoons coriander leaves
2 tablespoons chopped onion
2 tablespoons fat

Cook peas in boiling salted water with the coriander leaves. Fry onion in fat. Add peas and cook for 5 minutes.

Ejotes (Green Beans)

1 pound green beans
1 cup diced salt pork
1 small onion, chopped
1 clove garlic, chopped

2 cups tomatoes
Pinch of nutmeg
1 tablespoon chile powder
Salt

Snap and cut beans. Cook in enough water to keep from scorching. Fry salt pork, removing all fat except 4 tablespoons. Add onion and garlic to fat and salt pork. Cook until onion is done. Add cooked beans, tomatoes, nutmeg, chile powder, and salt. Boil for 10 or 15 minutes.

Cocido de Garbanzo (Garbanzo Stew)

1 cup garbanzos
6 cups water
1 small onion, sliced
1 clove garlic, chopped

1 cup chopped ham
1 cup Spanish sausage
1 teaspoon oregano
Salt and pepper, to taste

Soak garbanzos overnight. Drain and add water. Cook, and when half done, add onion, garlic, ham, and sausage. Cook until garbanzos are tender. Add oregano, salt and pepper, and leave on stove over a slow fire until soup is thick. If desired, a chile pepper may be added for seasoning.

Frijoles (Beans)

We have two varieties of beans which are popular in New Mexico; the pinto, a spotted bean, and the bolita, a round brown bean. The bolita, which cooks more quickly at high altitudes, is a native of the high mountain farm land. The pinto grows in a semi-arid climate and is a harder bean to cook. In the diet the pinto is, at low cost, an excellent source of energy, of iron, and the B complex vitamins. When supplemented with small amounts of milk, meat, eggs, or cheese, it is a good source of protein. It is also a good source of calcium.

The secret of tasty beans lies in cooking them just right. They must be cooked at low temperature and for a long time. An earthenware pot is the best utensil, but metal kettles may be used successfully.

1 cup beans	4 tablespoons fat or ½ cup diced
5 cups water	salt pork
1 clove garlic	Salt, to taste
1 teaspoon sugar	

Wash and soak beans overnight. Cook in boiling water, adding garlic and sugar at the beginning. If beans dry, add boiling water each time. It takes from 3 to 6 hours to cook them, depending on altitude and softness of the water. (If salt pork is used add after beans have cooked for at least one-half hour.) When beans are done, add fat and salt. Cook a few minutes to bring out the flavor.

Note The pressure cooker may be used successfully in cooking beans. The bolitas cook in 45 minutes and the pintos in 1 hour, at 15 pounds pressure. After pressure has been released, uncover kettle and cook beans for at least 20 minutes to remove the pressure cooker flavor which many people find objectionable.

Variation To make Frijoles Machacados (Mashed Beans), make sure beans are well-cooked and the liquid reduced to the point that there will not be any surplus to make beans watery. Mash beans lightly with potato masher. Melt 2 tablespoons fat, add 2 tablespoons flour, and brown, pour beans into it, salt. Cook for 5 to 10 minutes, stirring frequently.

Frijoles Refritos (Refried Beans)

Leftover beans lose their flavor unless fat is added. Melt enough fat for the amount of beans on hand. Fry until thoroughly incorporated with the grease. Enough grated cheese to flavor the refritos may be added. It requires very little cooking, as the cheese immediately melts when added to the hot mixture.

Papas y Chile (Potatoes and Chile)

2 small onions, chopped fine
4 tablespoons fat
1 cup canned green chile or freshly
  prepared Green Chile (page 17)

2 teaspoons salt
4 good-size potatoes, cooked and
  diced

Fry onions in fat until tender. Add green chile, salt, potatoes, and a small amount of water. Cook for 5 minutes.

Calabacitas con Chile Verde
(Summer Squash and Green Chile)

4 teaspoons fat
4 medium-size summer squashes
½ small onion, chopped
¼ cup milk

½ cup chopped cooked green chile
Salt and pepper
½ cup grated native or
  American cheese

Melt fat; add diced squash and onion. Fry until tender. When done, add milk, green chile, salt, and pepper. Cook 15 minutes. Remove from fire and add grated cheese.

Variation In place of green chile, 1 cup canned whole kernel corn may be added.

Pan de Papas (Potato Loaf)

Potatoes are best cooked in their skins.

4 eggs, separated	**1 clove garlic, chopped**
2 teaspoons salt	**2 tablespoons minced bacon**
1 teaspoon pepper	**4 cups cooked and diced potatoes**
½ cup milk	**2 tablespoons olive oil**

Beat egg whites until stiff; add beaten yolks, salt, pepper, milk, garlic, and bacon. Fold potatoes into egg mixture. Put olive oil into baking dish. Pour mixture into dish and bake until egg sets.

Ensalada de Berro (Watercress Salad)

Wash watercress carefully. Chop a small onion. Rub bowl with garlic. Combine ingredients, place in bowl, and serve with French dressing.

Verdolagas (Purslane)

3 cups purslane
2 tablespoons chopped onion
4 tablespoons fat or ½ cup diced
  salt pork

1 cup shredded cooked meat
  (jerky preferred)
1 teaspoon ground coriander seed
Salt, to taste

Wash purslane, leaving stems. Fry onion in fat; add purslane and meat. Season. Cover and cook until tender.

Quelites (Lamb's Quarters)

We have many wild greens which are prepared for the table. The best flavored is lamb's quarters; but pig weed, bee weed, and others may be used as well.

2 tablespoons fat
2 tablespoons chopped onion
2 cups chopped, cooked greens

1 tablespoon chile seed
½ cup cooked pinto or bolita beans
1 teaspoon salt

Place fat in skillet, fry chopped onion, add chopped greens, season with chile seeds, cooked beans (cooked whole), and salt.

Variation Salt pork cut fine may be used for frying, leaving it in for flavor.

Chiles Encurtidos (Pickled Chiles)

Select small chile pods. The wax chile is preferred by many. Wash chile pods carefully. Put into sterilized jars, packing tightly. To every pint jar add $\frac{1}{2}$ teaspoon whole mixed spices and enough vinegar to cover. Remove the air bubbles by passing knife around inside of jar. Seal jars. Process in hot water bath for 10 minutes.

Variation A brine made by adding 1 teaspoon of salt to 1 cup of water may be used to dilute the vinegar. Use 1 cup of vinegar and 1 cup of brine and you may like the resulting product better than with strong vinegar.

Ensalada de Aguacate (Avocado Salad)

1 clove garlic
1 large firm avocado
2 fresh tomatoes
4 radishes

1 small onion
1 small head of lettuce
Salt
French dressing

Rub bowl thoroughly with garlic. Dice avocado and place in bowl. Cut tomatoes in cubes and drain. Chop radishes and onion, shred lettuce, and combine with other ingredients. Chill. When ready to serve, add chilled French dressing.

Ensalada de Col y Cebolla
(Cabbage and Onion Salad)

1 clove garlic
2 cups shredded cabbage

1 onion, shredded
French dressing

Rub bowl with garlic. Mix cabbage and onion with French dressing. Stir well.

Ensalada de Coliflor (Cauliflower Salad)

1 head cauliflower
½ cup oil
1 clove garlic, chopped

¼ teaspoon ground chile
¼ cup vinegar

Separate cauliflower into flowerlets. Cook for 5 minutes in salted water. Drain. Heat oil; add garlic, ground chile, and vinegar; let come to a boil. Cool. Place cauliflower on lettuce leaves and cover with sauce.

Ensalada de Frijol (Pinto Bean Salad)

2 cups cooked pinto beans
½ cup diced celery
3 green chile peppers (canned
  or fresh)
2 medium cucumber pickles, chopped

½ small onion, chopped
Salt
Pepper
2 tablespoons prepared mustard
4 tablespoons cream or canned milk

Mix all ingredients thoroughly except mustard and cream. Beat mustard and cream together. Add to the bean mixture. Serve on lettuce. Sprinkle top with red chile powder.

Ensalada de Lechuga (Lettuce Salad)

1 head lettuce	2 tablespoons vinegar
1 small onion, chopped fine	1 teaspoon chile powder
1 clove garlic	Salt
4 tablespoons olive oil	Pepper

Remove core from lettuce. Pour cold water over it. The leaves will come apart. Drain. Chop lettuce and add onion. Put the other ingredients in jar or bottle and shake until well mixed.

Note If the garlic is used with the oil dressing, prepare dressing at least 6 hours before using, so that the garlic flavor may be absorbed by the other ingredients. The garlic, however, may be used to rub the serving bowl if the salad is to be served that way.

Cocktail de Aguacate (Avocado Cocktail)

Select 4 small avocados which are firm, cut into small squares (about $1/4$ inch). Prepare sauce as follows: 1 cup catsup, 1 cup diced celery, 2 tablespoons lemon juice or 1 tablespoon vinegar, 4 drops Tabasco sauce, 1 teaspoon salt, 1 teaspoon sugar. Serve avocados in cocktail glasses and put 2 tablespoons of the prepared sauce over the avocados. Serves 12.

Ensalada Mexicana (Mexican Salad)

3 large green sweet peppers
1 medium onion
4 medium ripe tomatoes

4 slices of bacon
1 teaspoon chile powder
½ cup vinegar

Cut vegetables in small chunks and mix. Cut bacon in small strips and cook crisp in hot skillet. Stir in chile powder and add the vinegar. As it boils up, pour over the vegetables. Serve on lettuce leaves.

Jalapeños Encurtidos (Pickled Jalapeños)

The jalapeño is a hot green pepper native of warm climates. It make a delicious relish pickled in olive oil and vinegar.

Wash jalapeño peppers. Pack tightly in jar. For every cup of vinegar use ¼ cup water, ¼ cup olive oil, 1 teaspoon salt, and 1 teaspoon pickling spices. Heat mixture to boiling. Pour over peppers so that they are well-covered. Seal jars. Process 10 minutes in hot water bath.

SOPAS, PANES Y EMPAREDADOS
(SOUPS, BREAD, AND SANDWICHES)

Sopa de Chícharos (Pea Soup)

The recipe given here is for dry pea soup. For variation, dry chick peas or beans may be substituted.

1 cup dried peas	2 teaspoons salt
6 cups boiling water	1 tablespoon fat
1 small onion, sliced	2 cups milk
1 clove garlic	

Cook peas with onion, garlic, and salt in water until peas are well-done. Pass through colander, using all the liquid. Add fat and milk and cook until thoroughly heated.

Sopa de Verduras (Vegetable Soup)

1 soup bone
6 cups water
1 cup green beans
3 small squashes
½ onion

1 red chile pod
1 clove garlic
1 teaspoon dry mint
2 teaspoons salt

Cook soup bone in water. When meat is cooked, strain soup. Add beans, squashes, onion, chile pod, and garlic to soup. Cook until beans are done. Add mint and salt. Serve.

Buñuelos (Fried Tortillas)

Often erroneously called sopaipillas.

4 cups flour
1 teaspoon salt
4 teaspoons baking powder

2 tablespoons fat
1 ½ cups water (about)
Vegetable fat, for frying

Sift flour, salt, and baking powder together. Work fat into flour until well-blended. Add enough water to make a soft dough but not sticky. Knead well; let stand for at least ½ hour. Form into round balls, roll ⅛ inch thick in round shapes or roll dough in a long strip and cut into 3-inch squares. Fry in deep fat (365 degrees F.) until brown, dropping each buñuelo in the hottest part of the fat. Drain.

Tortillas de Trigo (Wheat Tortillas)

2 cups white flour
2 cups whole-wheat native flour
1 ½ teaspoons salt
4 teaspoons baking powder

4 tablespoons fat
1 cup water, or enough to make
 medium dough

Sift flours, salt, and baking powder together; add fat and mix well. Add water. Knead dough for 5 minutes. Let stand ½ hour covered. Form into round, flat balls; and roll with rolling pin into a round shape about ⅛ inch thick. Cook on griddle, on top of stove, or in the oven. Brown on both sides.

Note All white flour may be used.

Bollitos (Rolls)

2 yeast cakes
½ cup lukewarm water
1 ½ cups milk
4 tablespoons fat

1 teaspoon salt
2 tablespoons sugar
6 to 8 cups flour

Soak yeast in lukewarm water. Place milk in a pan on top of stove. Add fat, salt, and sugar; and leave until fat is melted. Cool to lukewarm. Add yeast, mixing well. Add flour gradually until a medium dough results. Let rise until double in bulk. Form dough into balls, patting into rounds about 2 ½ inches in diameter. Fold in half. Place on a greased pan. Grease rolls on top. Let rise until double in size. Bake in hot oven until brown on both sides.

Tip To make Bizcocho (Toasted Rolls), break rolls in half, place in a slow oven, and toast until dry and crisp. Store to use with sopa (soup) or Hormiguillo (page 105).

Variation To make Molletes (Sweet Rolls), make dough as for rolls and let rise. Then to this dough add 2 beaten eggs, 1 cup sugar, 2 teaspoons anise seed, and 3 tablespoons fat. Shape into round rolls. Let rise for 1 hour. Bake in hot oven. Slice and butter to serve with chocolate, coffee, or tea.

Emparedado de Aguacate (Avocado Sandwich)

4 tablespoons grated cheese
1 cup mashed avocado
2 tablespoons chopped green chile
1 tablespoon catsup

2 drops Tabasco sauce
1 teaspoon salt
1 teaspoon chopped onion
Lettuce

Mash cheese; add avocado mixed with other ingredients; blend well; spread between slices of bread with lettuce leaves.

Emparedado de Frijol (Bean Sandwich)

1 cup cooked beans
2 tablespoons finely chopped onion
2 tablespoons chopped green chile

2 tablespoons chopped sour pickles
1 tablespoon prepared mustard
Lettuce

Mash beans, and add other ingredients, and spread on bread with lettuce leaves.

Emparedado de Queso y Chile Verde
(Cheese and Green Chile Sandwich)

Toast one side of bread slices; slice cheese thin to fit slice of bread; place cheese on untoasted side of bread, cover with finely chopped green chile. Place under the broiler or in oven and toast until cheese melts.

Machitos (Bean and Tortilla Sandwich)

Spread a wheat or corn tortilla with leftover beans which have been seasoned with pork cracklings. Fold tortilla and serve.

Tacos (Tortillas Filled with Meat)

8 corn tortillas (see page 21)
1 pound of boiling meat (pork or beef)
2 cloves garlic, chopped
2 teaspoons oregano
1 tablespoon parsley

1 cup cooked diced potatoes
2 cups Chile Sauce I, of choice (page 14)
1 small onion
1 small head of lettuce

Prepare tortillas. Fry and fold in center. Cook meat and grind. Add seasonings, potatoes and chile to ground meat. Boil until quite thick. Place meat mixture, diced onion, and shredded lettuce between folded tortillas. Serve with more sauce if desired.

POSTRES, PASTAS Y GOLOSINAS
(DESSERTS, PASTRIES, AND SWEETS)

Arroz en Leche (Rice in Milk)

1 cup rice
5 cups water
1 teaspoon salt
4 cups scalded milk

2 beaten eggs
1 cup sugar
Cinnamon

Cook rice in boiling, salted water until it begins to swell. Drain. Add hot milk and eggs, stir in sugar, and continue cooking until well-done. Serve in dessert dishes. Sprinkle top with cinnamon.

Torrejas Enmeladas (Sweet Fritters)

1 cup sugar
2 cups water
1 teaspoon cinnamon

1 batch Torrejas (Egg Fritters)
(page 59)

Caramelize sugar. Add water and cinnamon. Boil until sugar dissolves. Drop egg fritters into syrup. Let stand until the fritters are coated with sugar. Serve hot as dessert.

Natillas (Boiled Custard)

4 cups milk
4 eggs

3 tablespoons flour
¾ cup sugar
½ teaspoon salt

Heat the milk. Beat egg whites until stiff. Pour into hot milk, being careful that milk does not boil over. When egg whites are cooked, skim off from milk and place in a serving bowl. Mix flour, sugar, salt, and beaten egg yolks; and add to hot milk. Cook until thick. Pour into egg whites and sprinkle top with cinnamon.

Flan (Custard)

1 ½ cups sugar, divided
4 eggs

¼ teaspoon salt
1 tall can evaporated milk
1 teaspoon vanilla

Heat 1 cup sugar in casserole or mold until dark brown syrup is formed. Turn the container so that the syrup coats bottom and sides.

Beat eggs lightly. Add ½ cup sugar, salt, milk, and vanilla. Mix thoroughly. Pour into casserole or container coated with caramel. Cover. Set in pan of hot water and cook for 1 hour, or until a knife inserted in the center of the custard comes out clean. Serves 6.

Capirotada (Bread Pudding)

1 cup sugar
2 cups water
1 teaspoon cinnamon
6 slices toasted bread

1 ½ cups grated or sliced cheese
1 cup raisins
2 tablespoons butter

Caramelize sugar, add water and cinnamon, and boil until sugar is dissolved. Place a layer of bread in a casserole; add cheese and raisins. Repeat until all ingredients are used. Add butter. Pour syrup over mixture and bake in moderate oven until the syrup is all absorbed by bread.

Panocha (Sprouted Wheat Dessert)

The flour may be prepared at home or bought already prepared. To sprout wheat, wash and drain but do not dry it. Place in a cloth bag in a warm place to sprout. When the wheat has sprouted, dry in sun. Grind into flour.

5 cups sprouted wheat flour
2 ½ cups whole-wheat flour
9 cups boiling water

2 cups sugar (if desired)
4 tablespoons butter

Mix the sprouted and whole wheat flour thoroughly, add one half of the boiling water, and stir well. Set aside and cover. Let stand for 15 minutes; then add the rest of the water. If sugar is used, caramelize the sugar, add 1 cup boiling water, and when sugar is dissolved, add to flour mixture. Boil mixture for 2 hours, add butter and place uncovered in oven for 1 hour or until it is quite thick and deep brown. Some people prefer to leave sugar out, as the sprouted wheat has its own sugar.

Empanaditas de Carne (Meat Turnovers)

Mincemeat

1 pound boiling meat, cooked
1 ½ cups raisins
2 cups applesauce or jam
1 cup sugar
1 teaspoon ground coriander seed
½ teaspoon ground cloves
1 teaspoon cinnamon
1 teaspoon salt
½ cup shelled piñon nuts

Dough

1 cake yeast
1 ½ cups water or milk
3 tablespoons fat
1 ½ teaspoons salt
2 tablespoons sugar
Flour

Mincemeat

Grind meat, add raisins, applesauce, sugar, spices, and nuts. If the mixture is too dry, add a little of the meat stock, but be careful that the paste is not soft. It should be moist but thick in consistency. Make dough for turnovers as follows.

Dough

Soak yeast in ¼ cup lukewarm water. Heat water or milk; add fat, salt, and sugar. Cool to lukewarm and add dissolved yeast. Add enough flour to make a medium dough. Do not let rise. Roll out dough to $\frac{1}{8}$ inch thick. Cut with biscuit cutter. If the dough rises after the biscuits are cut, roll them thin. Place $1\frac{1}{2}$ teaspoons of mincemeat in center of rolled-out dough, fold and pinch together; then make a turn back in the dough by taking edges between thumb and forefinger, pressing together and turning back in ridges.

Let turnovers stand for 5 minutes; then fry in deep fat until evenly browned. Makes about 8 dozen.

Calabaza al Horno I (Baked Pumpkin)

1 small pumpkin
1 cup sugar
1 teaspoon salt

Remove seeds from pumpkin. Cut into 2-inch squares, leaving shell on. Place pieces in baking dish. Sprinkle with sugar and salt. Bake until pulp is soft. Serve in shell with boiled milk.

Calabaza al Horno II (Baked Pumpkin)

1 small pumpkin
2 cups sugar

1 teaspoon salt
2 cups milk

Remove seeds from pumpkin. Peel and cut into 2-inch cubes. Place in baking dish. Sprinkle with sugar and salt. Add milk. Cook in moderate oven until done. It may be necessary to add more milk to keep pumpkin from drying.

Bizcochitos (Cookies)

2 cups lard
1 cup sugar
1 teaspoon anise seed
2 eggs

6 cups sifted flour
3 teaspoons baking powder
1 teaspoon salt
$\frac{1}{4}$ cup water

Cream lard with hand thoroughly; add sugar and anise seed. Beat eggs and add to lard mixture. Blend until light and fluffy. Sift flour with baking powder and salt and add to first mixture. Add water and knead until well-mixed. Roll $\frac{1}{2}$ inch thick and cut into fancy shapes. Roll top of each cookie in a mixture of sugar and cinnamon—1 teaspoon cinnamon to $\frac{1}{2}$ cup sugar. Bake in a moderate oven until slightly brown.

Empanadas de Fruta (Fruit Turnovers)

1 ½ cups flour
1 teaspoon baking powder
1 teaspoon salt
8 tablespoons shortening
4 to 6 tablespoons water

Fruit Filling
2 cups cooked dried fruit
1 cup sugar
1 teaspoon cinnamon
½ teaspoon ground cloves

Sift flour with baking powder and salt. Cut in shortening and mix well. Add enough water to make a dough easy to handle. Roll out dough ⅛ inch thick. Cut in rounds about 3 inches in diameter. Fill each round with fruit filling.

To make the fruit filling, pass drained fruit through colander. (Canned, drained fruit may be used.) Add sugar and spices. Press edges of filled dough and pinch ends between thumb and forefinger, giving the dough half a turn. Bake in hot oven until brown.

Marquesote (Sponge Cake)

8 eggs
1 cup pulverized sugar

2 teaspoons anise seed
10 tablespoons cornstarch

Beat egg whites until stiff, and add sugar and anise seed. Beat egg yolks and add corn starch. Add egg yolk mixture to egg white mixture, beating constantly. Pour into ungreased cake pan to one-half full. Bake in moderate oven.

Sopaipillas (Sweet Fried Cakes)

These are nice cakes for serving with chocolate or tea.

4 cups flour
1 teaspoon salt
2 teaspoons baking powder
4 tablespoons fat

4 eggs
1/2 cup sugar
Water or milk

Sift flour with salt and baking powder. Cut fat into flour. Beat eggs, add sugar, and add to flour mixture. Add enough water or milk to make a medium dough neither stiff nor soft. Let dough stand for 1/2 hour. Roll out 1/4 inch thick, cut into 1 1/2 inch squares and fry in deep fat until brown.

To 1/2 cup of sugar, add 1 teaspoon cinnamon and mix well. As the sopaipillas are fried and drained and still hot, roll in the sugar and cinnamon mixture.

Enmeladas (Fried Cakes in Syrup)

Make Sopaipillas as in the preceding recipe. After they have been fried, dip into syrup.

Syrup

6 cups sugar
3 cups water
1 teaspoon cinnamon

Caramelize sugar. When melted and brown add water. Cook until thick. Add cinnamon, mixing well. Each sopaipilla is dipped separately into the syrup and taken out immediately. Drain on platter. Serve as dessert.

Jamoncillo (Cream Candy)

1 cup sugar
2 cups milk

Boil sugar and milk slowly until thick and medium brown in color. This makes delicious sweet sandwiches.

If desired, the sugar and milk can be boiled to the hard ball stage. When done, pour into buttered dish and cut into squares.

Cajeta de Membrillo (Quince Cheese)

5 pounds quince
5 pounds sugar

Wash and core quince, remove seeds, quarter, and cover with water. Cook until fruit is soft. Pass through colander. Place in kettle and add sugar. Cook until thick and dark red in color. Stir frequently to prevent scorching. When done, pour into molds. After it cools, take out of mold, cover with cheese cloth and set in sun to dry. When dry, wrap in waxed paper and store.

Variation To make Dulces de Membrillo (Quince Candy), slice Quince Cheese in slices $1/8$ inch thick. Spread on waxed paper and place to dry. When dry, roll in powdered sugar.

Ponte Duro (Caramelized Corn)

Use white corn, preferably the concho variety. Toast corn in a skillet until brown. When done, pour hot corn syrup over the corn, and let boil. When cool enough to handle, shape into balls.

Conserva de Calabaza (Pumpkin Preserve)

The best variety of pumpkin to use is the native New Mexican, a long necked pumpkin, green and yellow striped, which is very firm and holds its shape.

Cut pumpkin; remove seeds. Cut into cubes and peel. Place cubes in lime solution to the proportion of 4 tablespoons of lime to each gallon of water. Be sure lime water covers pumpkin cubes. Let stand for 12 hours. Drain, wash thoroughly. Weigh. Add as much sugar by weight as there is pumpkin. Let stand with sugar for at least one hour. When juice begins to show, place over low heat, and cook until pumpkin is done and has become dark brown and transparent.

Variation Pumpkin Preserve cubes may be dried to make Dulces de Calabaza (Pumpkin Candy). Take the pumpkin cubes out of the syrup. Lay on waxed paper and place in the sun to dry. Turn frequently. When no moisture shows, the candy is ready.

BEBIDAS
(BEVERAGES)

Most of the recipes given here are for drinks usually served to sick or old people, or to children. They are light nutritious foods.

Atole (Gruel)

½ cup blue corn meal
2 cups boiling water

Stir corn meal in ¹/₂ cup cold water, add to boiling water. Boil until it has reached the consistency of cream. Cook. Serve in cups about half full. Add enough salted boiled milk to fill cups. This is a very common beverage for sick or old people.

Champurrado (Chocolate in Atole)

2 squares spiced chocolate or
  Mexican chocolate
¹/₄ cup boiling water

2 cups of Atole or Polvillo
  (page 103)

Dissolve chocolate in boiling water. Add to Atole or Polvillo. Sweeten to taste.

Chocolate (Chocolate)

1 quart milk
1 (1-inch) stick cinnamon
3 tablespoons strong coffee
2 squares sweet chocolate

½ cup boiling water
1 tablespoon vanilla
⅛ teaspoon salt
½ teaspoon nutmeg

Heat milk to boiling with cinnamon and coffee. Remove cinnamon and add chocolate dissolved in boiling water. Heat again to boiling. Remove from fire, and add vanilla and salt. Beat with egg beater or molinillo (chocolate beater) until foamy.

Variation If commercially prepared Mexican chocolate is used, proceed as follows: To 1 quart cold milk add 2 squares of chocolate dissolved in 1 cup boiling water. Keep over fire until it comes to a boil. Beat with egg beater or chocolate beater.

Pinole (Corn Meal Drink)

4 tablespoons corn meal
½ teaspoon cinnamon
1 cup milk

2 tablespoons brown sugar
1 tablespoon ground orange rind

Mix corn meal and cinnamon. Stir into cold milk, add sugar and orange rind. Stir well and serve.

Note To be palatable, the corn meal must be made from toasted corn. In New Mexico the native corn meal is always ground from toasted corn.

Poleadas (Flour Gruel)

2 tablespoons flour
2 tablespoons sugar
1 cup boiling water

1 teaspoon salt
½ teaspoon anise seed

Mix flour and sugar thoroughly, and dissolve in a little water. Add to the boiling water. Stir until it thickens. Add salt and anise seed.

Polvillo (Toasted Flour Gruel)

Toast wheat flour in oven until brown. Stir constantly while browning or it will scorch. Any amount may be browned, for it will keep indefinitely if kept in a jar covered with cheese cloth.

6 tablespoons browned flour
4 teaspoons cold water

2 cups boiling water
White or brown sugar

Dissolve flour in cold water, pour into boiling water, and cook thoroughly. Sweeten with sugar to taste.

Cocktail de Jugo de Tomatoes
(Tomato Juice Cocktail)

2 cups tomato juice
1 teaspoon salt
$\frac{1}{8}$ teaspoon celery salt

$\frac{1}{2}$ teaspoon red chile powder
1 tablespoon onion juice
1 tablespoon lemon juice

Boil tomato juice with spices and onion juice. Strain and cool. Add lemon juice.
Serve in glasses and top with a sprig of mint.

Hormiguillo (Hard-Tack Gruel)

Take 6 pieces of Bizcocho (page 80) and grind fine like flour. Add a pinch each of ground oregano, coriander, cloves, and cinnamon. Sift. Place 2 cups water to boil. Slowly add 4 tablespoons of the ground bizcocho mixture. Boil until thick. Sweeten and salt to taste.

Café con Leche (Coffee with Milk)

Make coffee good and strong. Heat milk to boiling (goat's milk preferred). Fill coffee cups $1/4$ full with hot coffee. Fill with milk and serve.

MENUS

Menus for Luncheons

Emparedados de Queso y Chile Verde / Green Chile Sandwiches
Frijoles Refritos / Refried Beans
Chocolate con Sopaipillas / Chocolate with Fried Sweet Cakes

Ensalada de Aguacate / Avocado Salad
Sopa Seca de Arroz / Dry Rice Soup
Café con Leche / Coffee and Milk
Natillas / Boiled Custard

Sopa de Garbanzo / Garbanzo Soup
Emparedados de Aguacate / Avocado Sandwiches
Pinole / Corn Meal Drink
Arroz en Leche / Rice in Milk

Tacos / Tortillas Filled with Meat
Frijoles / Beans
Café con Leche / Coffee with Milk
Fruta / Fruit

Ensalada de Frijol / Bean Salad
Torrejas con Chile / Chile Fritters
Buñuelos / Fried Tortillas
Queso Fresco con Mermelada / Fresh Cheese with Marmalade

Sopa de Chícharos / Pea Soup
Ensalada Mexicana / Mexican Salad
Tortillas de Trigo / Wheat Tortillas
Chocolate con Bizcochitos / Chocolate with Cookies

Tamales
Ensalada de Lechuga / Lettuce Salad
Salsa de Chile I / Chile Sauce I
Buñuelos / Fried Tortillas
Café con Leche / Coffee with Milk
Piña Envasada / Canned Pineapple

Menus for Dinners

Cocktail de Jugo de Tomatoes / Tomato Juice Cocktail
Pozole de Nixtamal / Lime Hominy with Meat
Cajeta de Membrillo / Quince Cheese
Ensalada de Col y Cebolla / Cabbage and Onion Salad
Café con Leche / Coffee with Milk
Buñuelos / Fried Tortillas

Enchiladas con Huevo / Enchiladas with Egg
Ensalada de Lechuga / Lettuce Salad
Frijoles Machacados / Mashed Beans
Bollitos / Hot Rolls
Café con Leche / Coffee with Milk
Durazno Envasado / Canned Peaches

Ensalada de Berro / Watercress Salad
Albondigas / Meat Balls
Pan de Papas / Potato Loaf
Chícharos Verdes / Green Peas
Tortillas de Trigo / Wheat Tortillas
Torrejas Enmeladas / Sweet Fritters

Cocktail de Aguacate / Avocado Cocktail
Pollo Frito / Fried Chicken
Bollitos / Hot Rolls
Calabacitas con Chile Verde / Green Squash with Green Chile
Café con Leche / Coffee with Milk
Flan / Custard

Lenten Menus

Sopa de Garbanzo / Garbanzo Soup
Pescado Relleno / Stuffed Fish
Ensalada de Coliflor / Cauliflower Salad
Papas y Chile / Potatoes and Chile
Tortillas de Maiz / Corn Tortillas
Peras Envasadas / Canned Pears

Torrejas de Camaron / Shrimp Fritters
Chícharos Maduros / Dried Mature Peas
Ensalada de Lechuga / Lettuce Salad
Bollitos / Hot Rolls
Panocha / Sprouted Wheat Dessert
Café con Leche / Coffee with Milk

Sopa de Frijol / Bean Soup
Pescado Frito / Fried Fish
Ensalada de Aguacate / Avocado Salad
Capirotada / Bread Pudding
Chicos Quebrados con Chile / Cracked Chicos with Chile
Pan / Bread
Café con Leche / Coffee with Milk

Tortilla Española / Spanish Omelet
Chile Verde Guisado / Green Chile
Buñuelos / Fried Tortillas
Ensalada de Berro / Watercress Salad
Chongos / Cheese Twists
Chocolate / Chocolate

Sopa de Garbanzo / Garbanzo Soup
Torrejas con Chile / Corn Fritters
Frijoles / Beans
Quelites / Lamb's Quarters
Tortillas de Trigo / Wheat Tortillas
Arroz con Leche / Rice with Milk
Café con Leche / Coffee with Milk

Meriendas (Teas) Menu

Chocolate / Chocolate
Empanadas de Carne / Mincemeat Turnovers
Bizcochitos / Cookies
Dulces de Calabaza / Pumpkin Candy

Champurrado / Chocolate in Atole
Sopaipillas / Fried Sweet Cakes
Emparedados de Jamoncillo / Cream Candy Sandwiches

Te o Café / Tea or Coffee
Molletes con Mantequilla / Sweet Rolls with Butter
Emparedados de Aguacate / Avocado Sandwiches
Chocolate / Chocolate
Dulces de Membrillo / Quince Candy
Marquesote / Sponge Cake

Café con Leche / Coffee with Milk
Tamales
Bizcochitos / Cookies

INDEX

Metric Conversion Chart

Volume Measurements		Weight Measurements		Temperature Conversion	
U.S.	Metric	U.S.	Metric	Fahrenheit	Celsius
1 teaspoon	5 ml	1/2 ounce	15 g	250	120
1 tablespoon	15 ml	1 ounce	30 g	300	150
1/4 cup	60 ml	3 ounces	90 g	325	160
1/3 cup	75 ml	4 ounces	115 g	350	180
1/2 cup	125 ml	8 ounces	225 g	375	190
2/3 cup	150 ml	12 ounces	350 g	400	200
3/4 cup	175 ml	1 pound	450 g	425	220
1 cup	250 ml	2 1/4 pounds	1 kg	450	230